THE NEW BURNING TIMES

THERE ARE NO WITCHES

Tarl Warwick
2019

COPYRIGHT AND DISCLAIMER

INTRODUCTION

They say hindsight is 20-20. It is with this in mind that I end this decade with one final authored work; a short, sweet reflection on some of the most manifestly nonsensical ravings of the authoritarian species which have taken place over the last few years. A slow, seeping poison is gradually sickening the western world as we speak; the sickness of totalitarianism. I am as ever optimistic about mankind, about our chances as a species *per se*, even if eventually we will be wiped out by an asteroid or some similar natural calamity- I do not believe mankind will destroy itself (even if it actively attempts it- sometimes it certainly seems to be the case.)

However, for those of us who believe life is not fundamentally worth living without some semblance of liberty, it is a bleak world indeed. Empty spaces, once inhabited by a few loners who did not wish to be under the yoke of tyranny, are all but gone, and even spaces of a non-physical character- prior a land of fantasy and imagination and progress technologically- are being sanitized and everything within turned into proprietary material so that dissent can be actively snuffed out by billionaires and governments at a whim.

I speak of the internet; a refuge ten years ago for independent content creation, unique and foreword thought- now a cesspit of witch hunting devolved from its lofty heights by the active intrusion of morons and opportunists, and hivelike hordes of well meaning but delusional pearl clutchers and busybodies easily swayed to believe whatever a newspaper tells them. And tell them they have; they have lied openly to the population, told it that some random podcast or a video game reviewer with a social media presence is the reason the world is bad and ugly, or is responsible for the latest shooting.

THE NEW BURNING TIMES

This is of course utter nonsense. Reasonable people are unfortunately uncommon. Declare to these mind slaves that they have been opportunistically fooled by propaganda crafted by the same competitors of those independent voices and entrepreneurs and despite the claim being both reasonable and *observably* true, their eyes will glaze over, and they will be unable to process the point. Yes, they have been lied to- it hurts the much more because they are not evil or bad, merely misled by people who have ill intentions.

The concept that the internet- or culture in general, especially with regards to the technological zeitgeist of this era- is crowded by extremists, is patently, observably false. These propagandists with their lies have, however, managed to get around this by creating dense, legalistic studies of no merit, funneling them through "activistic" groups and media conglomerates. So long as each group borrows from and sources another, nobody can question the content- who is John Doe to argue with the New York Times, even if the source it uses is utterly discredited? After all, you wouldn't want to *disparage the rights of the press* would you?

We have achieved a moment in time in which the corporate media (I refer to it as the legacy media, because it is useless for gleaning any real information on any meaningful subject anymore) loves to utilize that excuse for its lies- and when caught out, it merely shrugs and ignores the issue or retracts it silently. The press was also utilized to crank out copies of the *Malleus Maleficarum* or "Hammer of the Witches"- that famous tract of nonsense circa the burning times, so long ago. Its contents were never seriously challenged so long as the burning fires were more than mere embers- hindsight indeed is 20-20. A century from now people will look back at the claims of the corporate press and its "activist" and political allies and they will be seen as no different from inquisitors or the residents of Salem.

THE NEW BURNING TIMES

It is thus that I present this little work. I have seen people whose videos, books, songs, and writings I have enjoyed, scratched off of the internet and in some cases out of society, for the "crime" of witchcraft viz a viz the modern era; for the new witchcraft is nothing more than the original sin of independence itself, and persecution of the same is the same persecution we have, as an enlightened society, supposedly left behind us.

I call for enlightenment. I call for those who know reality as it really is to try how they may to enlighten others so that we can live in a better world; in which dissent is cherished as an act, not spurned as an activity of extremists. In which rebellion is seen as appropriate and sometimes justified- as it observably is. I call on the intellectual and the moralist alike to renounce the yoke of tyranny in favor of rational debate and open public discourse, and for society to place business where business belongs; in the habit of making money, and producing, not in the habit of policing opinions or acts, and certainly not erecting its own pulpit to preach morality to the masses; a poisoned morality that can only suppress, never promote peace or liberty.

Intelligent as we modern "witches" may be, we are now as always a minority, and it is in the hands of often well meaning but fooled bystanders- the apolitical, the skeptic, the questioner of morals, the mere centrist- in *their* hands that the fate of a society rests. If those of us who understand true freedom do nothing, our world will sink into darkness not seen since the Medieval era. The vlogger, the podcast star, the independently published writer, the webmaster and coder and blogger, the small town singing sensation, we are all witches, today.

WITCHES THEN AND NOW

While it is true that I am a pagan, and an occultist, I will do my best not to wax too poetic on this particular topic, since for those not already aware, it is necessary for me to adulate witches (as they really were) in the 16th and 17th century.

It is- we must first note- not entirely the case that the average (usually religious) European of that era was truly so rudimentary and uneducated as they are typically portrayed in common modern parlance. Surely, some were superstitious, ignorant, and illiterate in a literal sense; others were more prudent, more studious. I do not intend this work (or this section of the work) as a refutation of Christendom *per se*, I merely point to the well established role of religious and religion-influenced moralism and authority in the era and the juxtaposed existence at the time of those on the edge of such society which had certain skills which made them targets.

If one reads the *Malleus Maleficarum* or similar works they will at once perhaps appreciate how a skilled herbal healer or crafty individual on the edge of society might be profiled a witch; the ability to dispense abortifacients (cohosh, pennyroyal, parsley, etc) alone was enough to show that a person was in league with the devil. Let us try and overlap that with modern times.

Then: Someone on the edge of society was profiled as a witch for having aberrant views or behaviors commensurate with what religious authorities deemed witchery. This made them dangerous. They were persecuted and sometimes destroyed.

Now: Someone reasoned to be on the edge of society is profiled as extreme for having aberrant views of behaviors commensurate with what corporate or political authorities deem to be extreme. This makes them dangerous. They are persecuted and their livelihood destroyed (in the modern world this can be little different than a death sentence.)

I am failing to see a great degree of difference between someone having years of work wiped out because the self-declared authorities of the "modern" era decide them to be dangerous, and someone four hundred years ago suffering a similar fate. I will answer a few miserable attempts by the authoritarians here directly.

They declare "but nobody is being killed! We are not trying to harm anyone, we are trying to save lives by preventing extremism!"

I answer: To deprive a person of their livelihood and announce to the world that they are extreme or remarkably dangerous is no different than rubbing them with a steak and placing them in a cage full of starving wolves. It is asinine to suggest that the declarations made by corporations today about the supposedly "extreme" at least amount to a dog whistle to the brainwashed to do all in their power to inconvenience, if not physically harm, the accused witch. Four hundred years ago, an "enlightened" town could spare the witch and simply cast her to the woods to scratch out a meager existence growing turnips. There aren't any such places now that are not digital; it is these digital fringe-lands being decimated by the same witch finders, ever hungry for more blood in their delusions of power. This rabble knows what it's doing. They do not fool me.

They declare "but it is the modern era! The mistakes of the past cannot therefore have any similarity with our enlightened era!"

I answer: The 1600s were modern in the 1600s. Our era seems very modern to us today, just as the citizen a hundred years ago witnessing the rise of art deco skyscrapers looked at the shining glass and marble, at the immaculate columns, the utter beauty of the tile, the trim, every expensive trinket, every rising dome and pillar of most ornate form, at the million lights of Paris or London, at the soaring skyline of New York, and they breathed whisperingly to themselves "this is modernity, this is the man, made godlike. All before was ignorance, all after will resemble this moment in time."

I recall not that many years ago living in a fairly small town in the relative backwater of Eastern Vermont, and we had manual parking meters, no internet connections, old school cash registers, and fifty cent candy bars. I am not even middle aged and that town has changed little, yet it is massively different. In my normal dwelling in Rutland, in Western Vermont- a town quite more sizable- change is even more extreme. I am in Amsterdam as I write this; I probably would be mentally unable to register the change if I had seen this city twenty years ago at the turn of the century and millennium.

Everyone is a child inside. The old man really feels, partly, like it is the time of his childhood. I was not fond of the 1990s so I am less nostalgic than most, but the feeling remains. There is *no such thing as modern*. There never will be. This bias and fallacy is ignorance.

They then say finally; "authorities have told us it is not as you state!"

I answer: I am the authority- because I recognize reality. Those others come in two varieties; we have the fool who means well, and the opportunist that means ill. Of these the former is arguably worse since someone who acts out of what they perceive of as righteousness will fight many times harder than someone who will cut their losses if their venomous evil becomes unprofitable or personally dangerous.

THE NEW BURNING TIMES

So there in a nutshell is the real truth: The population largely believed in witchcraft (if not in witches locally) centuries ago. When authorities wanted a scapegoat for why the world had issues, they found plenty of involuntary ones in the form of uncouth rural fringe-of-society dwellers, as well as the dregs of urban populations. The adulteress could be tossed on a pillory alongside the gypsy transient, the Jew, or the heretic. They were all, in a way, witches- and once debased as such, they were rendered subhuman in the minds of most. As I will later expound upon, even those who would have defended them usually did not, for fear of reprisal.

The population still believes in witches. The authorities of our supposedly modern time have simply found a new scapegoat that conforms to modern technology- really, modern communication. The abortion-dispensing old woman with her herb garden in 1623 is no longer even questioned by polite society; she is almost deified as a symbol of one of the few things that was "good" about the era. A victim, of folly.

I believe that centuries from now, people writing about our supposedly enlightened, modern time period, will say the same about those witches of today that dispense independent opinions and which inform and entertain from without the mainstream. About the sole difference we might legitimately register is that these days, we witches have a larger audience, which occasionally affords a little bit of protection; it's easier to be outspoken when you are not alone. But the corporate and political masters of today have spent years attempting to convince as many people as possible that todays vlogger or podcast star is a witch- a degenerated dreg malevolently attempting to harm society by promulgating violence or "fake" information- the same charge might more appropriately be leveled at the war lovers and propagandists of the same authorities making the claim.

SUPREMACY OF THE "RELIGIOUS" AUTHORITIES

Time passes but things remain the same as always. False appeals to authority are perhaps the greatest challenge in all eras- they are worse than appeals to actual authority, since the normal methods used to usurp abusive authority don't work so well when the authority itself is only an illusion.

We must first recognize that the religious figures of the burning times were mostly a political bloc merely set to a religious background. It would be difficult for any seasoned academic (even a religious one!) to argue that church authority- whether Catholic or Protestant- was not explicitly related to governance and order first and foremost- to lose the backing of the religion of ones' state meant being deposed, more often than not, to a leader, and cast out, if a noble, and killed, if less than that.

So it is today. The doctrines spun out like propagandistic spiders' webs to ensnare the dissenters of our time are considered self evidently factual, even when they are demonstrably false. The population by and large does not question what it is told- great for the oligarch or corporatist, terrible for everyone else- and while the public is no more gullible now than it has been, it is sadly also no less so. The false appeal to modernity runs deep and forms a cognitive dissonance in the minds of the populace, and they believe themselves to be too intelligent, too modern to be successfully lied to- especially about major things like there being an army of extremists out to traumatize their children and take over the world. But we will get to the patently nonsensical nature of such claims made in a subsequent section.

The church was, indeed, a political entity. So too are the corporate and activistic groups engaged in their nonsense today.

THE NEW BURNING TIMES

We must recognize that there is a fusion of church, state, corporation, and civilian organization, such that they run together and the lines between them are blurred. This was the case then, and now. And as always, since their corruption in this would be laid bare if people focused on identifying it, they cloak themselves with lurid claims of external foes.

Witches were the foe long ago. Sometimes, witches took a backseat because war broke out- the external foe that held society together (and allowed those in power to remain so outside of normal capitalistic competitive systems) was another state. In the west, communism in the eastern bloc held society together until the USSR collapsed. Since then, we have seen more and more internal incursions into day to day life- indeed, the death of the USSR and the availability of the internet to the civilian world both (coincidentally!) occur in 1991. Since that time, we have seen society condemn those who were different from the norm over and over again to cover its own problems up; a nonexistent trench coat mafia for example, or grunge rockers, or people on the internet who disagree with global neoliberalism and believe that some aspects of prior culture should be retained.

Attempts to make the claims of authority self evident are always undertaken because the authority itself is invariably too flimsy to stand up to scrutiny. If there is a gem of wisdom in recognizing this it is that *authoritarians operate out of fear and fragility*. Scrutiny shows them to be either fearful, or evil.

Today, Silicon Valley and the corporate for-profit press are treated as religious entities in an almost literal sense anyways. People practically worship at their Moloch-resembling altars. Even a pagan like myself can admit the irony of their malevolence which has begun to resemble some of the more frightening scenes of *Metropolis*.

As we speak right now, politicians are constantly

haranguing to their audiences that there is a "big problem" on the internet with "hate speech." That there is no designation for this term under US law seems largely ignored, which is sad since any scrutiny of the claim would cause massive laughter.

What has happened is that politicians are merely repeating the lies they got from the corporate press, which repeats them opportunistically since it helps them target and deplatform their independent competitors. The corporate media in turn got its sources from "activist" groups which mysteriously always seem to rub elbows with some combination of politicians, corporate media heads, or Silicon Valley corporate CEOs. The sources are normally bogus- I could write a separate book on that topic alone. Over the last few years I, the author, have been mentioned multiple times by corporate media groups, which have used blatantly politically biased website "sources" to show how I myself was "far right" or adjacent to "conspiracy theorists." These activistic groups are fond of extorting public figures out of money; the public figure either pays them to be left alone (since all of them too can be labeled "hateful" or "extreme" if enough mental gymnastics are done and there's a reason) or to get on their good side, because the leaders of such groups are well connected and wealthy.

This is an example of plutocrats helping one another out. The fact that self proclaimed "leftists" or "liberals" are the most given toward believing their corporatistic lies is more sad than amusing at this point.

WEIRD TALES

If I were to tell you that an old woman living on the edge of your town or city in a dilapidated trailer was in league with Satan because she suffered from cerebral palsy and muttered to herself, you would likely assume I was joking. If I pressed the issue, and continued to insist this to be the case, it's likely you'd think I was going funny in the head or was a fanatic. You'd be wrong; I'd actually be making a joke about the burning times!

Now, let's say I tell you that because someone is a vlogger and believes that postmodernism is bad, and that because of this, they are a nazi. Or let's say I claimed that they were a far right extremist because I saw them making the "OK" symbol with their hands, or let me just state that they must be on the "alt right" because they made a blog post five years prior in which they question the interchangeable nature of males and females. Would you react the same way as before?

For some the answer is "yes"- congratulations, you have gone past the modernity fallacy. The claims I am making are nonsensical, easily disproved to anyone not under the weight of self imposed cognitive dissonance, and cannot stand up to any serious scrutiny- but as we will see later in this manuscript, scrutiny is lacking, because most people have become afraid to scrutinize the claim anyways.

The claims made long ago about witches and witchcraft were fantastical in every way. The conception of a world populated by otherworldly entities both physical and super-physical led to the adoption of witches as the political scapegoat of the era. But now the super-physical has melted away. The rational world of "modern" times does not allow the devil to be blamed for societies problems. No; if there is no true external threat to blame problems on, some internal figure or group must be at fault, for polite society is just and good and rational, and would never be at fault for the evil of its members; yes, cognitive dissonance kicks in and these hyperbolic claims are subconsciously utilized by the populace and its masters alike.

Thank goodness, there are still witches!

I have heard the kookiest claims made by otherwise supposedly rational, even academically sophisticated individuals. I've even had them aimed at me. I initially reacted with bemused confusion before I realized the malevolent true mechanisms by which such dissonance had become commonplace. I have heard that milk- yes, *milk*, the drink, was potentially a hate symbol. I laughed- after all, I was there when the joke (for that is what it was) began; it was never a hate symbol- people having a lark pretended that it was, in order to get the self righteous, despicable "activists" of the era to latch onto the notion, thus proving themselves incapable of rational thought. It worked. The same joke was replicated in the guise of the "OK" symbol being used by "white supremacists." Lately, it has embroiled a group of Navy cadets in a "scandal" involving this patently ludicrous claim because they were playing a common game in which making the symbol is an invitation to get punched if you look at it.

The claims made today of armies of hateful or malevolent political figures and their supposed masters on social media sites are fantastical just like tales of armies of hellish demons whirling about at night possessing old women or hijacking infants for blood drinking Satanic rituals. The fact that people are unable to distinguish the ghoulish and phantasmagorical falsehoods of the 2010s is because they are hidden behind a faux veil of modernity and intellectual rigor. "New York Times" sounds more meaningfully respectable than "Ye Olde Witchfinder Tymes", but only because it "sounds rational."

THE NEW BURNING TIMES

We "witches"- for that is what all rational and independent minds are slowly being labeled- are the vanguard of real truth and reason in an era no more enlightened than any other. Centuries have passed but human biology and culture has changed little. The brief light of the enlightenment was all but extinguished in a hazy shroud of fire and brimstone fundamentalism the likes of which clung to the west until relatively modern times. And as soon as we threw off the shackles of religious persecution for what unfortunately is likely not the final time, we placed more manacles around us- this time calling them "reason" where there was none and "modernity" which does not exist. It is an illusion, a farce. All progress along these lines is an illusory falsehood.

I have communicated privately with people who are supposedly violent, or intellectually backwards, or despicably hateful, and I have *never* found any of them to be so in private. As a classical liberal of sorts (a libertarian, loosely, or a constitutionalist. I believe in liberty as a high value and fight for it. Whatever term you deem appropriate for one who primarily fights for liberty for oneself and others works.) I have defended these supposed dregs vigorously while also debating the finer points of their belief systems, which I often find as kooky as the kookiness of the supposedly polite, mainstream establishment (no more kooky, though!) In return I have been ridiculed as "empowering" or "platforming" extremism and hate, even though the individuals in question are, more often than not, not hateful to begin with. These linguistic propaganda tactics, these word games, are played solely to disparage people who are beyond the disparagement associated with them, to try and ridicule them as being subhuman and therefore unworthy of defending. And those of us who stand and defend them anyways are treated the same as the few advocates of the "witch" long ago, who often were persecuted subsequently alongside the "devil worshiping spawn of Satan" they wisely and morally tried to save from the gallows or the pillory.

COWARDS OF ALL AGES

Perhaps the most damning issue of all is the cowardice of the population. I do not mean this in an insulting manner; there are times I too worry. I defend liberty, but I am acutely aware that my foes are massively wealthy and corrupt and at a whim they can make my life difficult- try and perhaps succeed at disparaging me as a pariah, a lover of hate, as an extremist, making me an outcast, unable to ever hold what would be regarded as "normal" employment. If they want to put the screws to me even more, they can then pull a few strings and undercut my current form of income; my editing, my authoring of books like this one, they can attack my video making, my social media platforms, everywhere that I exist in the digital form.

It is a David and Goliath story played out over and over, century after century. Hindsight being 20-20, most of us pity the witch of the 17th century and condemn the witch finder. We are repulsed, usually, by the excess, the abuse of power, the feigned intelligentsia of the era with its leechcraft and stupid parlor tricks. We recognize it as the brutal, backwards, ignorant superstition it is.

How will history judge the fence sitter this time?

If the past is any indicator, the advocate of liberty, reason, and sense; the *neo-enlightened*, whether abused now or not, will be remembered fondly. I'd hate to be one of those voices silenced by fear, but silent often they remain. Most in society, I believe, now as before, understand that the central premise of a need for rich and powerful people to censor people like me to "stop hate" or "promote better dialogue" is newspeak propaganda and self serving corporate nonsense. This degenerated swill ideology is also deeply offensive, since it treats everyone as homogeneously stupid and unable to grasp basic reality. I know I, for my own part, am offended daily by what the corporate media and its cronies expect me to take at face value.

The number of people willing to argue in defense of witches accused long ago was pretty small; cowards that they were (for they were, indeed) the people backed off at the first sign of a witchfinder, and even aided their degeneracy by proclaiming even their own kin (contrary to their own patently observable knowledge) to be in league with dark forces, dooming their own siblings or friends, their own parents, children, local administrators, *even religious figures* to the fires of hell man-made by the superstitious zealots of the era. This last point is interesting; some who live by the sword die by it. I've even seen some of the independent voices that cheer on todays pillory stacked on a pyre like cordwood. All they need to do is offend one person, or be "wrong" on one topic, and they too get labeled "bigot"- the scarlet letter "B" of our time emblazoned on them for the world to see.

The masses are as much to blame for these moral panics as those who design them. I have laid out the basic progression before in non-literary form but will replicate it here:

1. Opportunists in positions of power generate a moral panic. This may be by political forces wishing to deflect their own issues, or religious orders seeking more alms, or corporate conglomerates who want more money.

2. The self-proclaimed truth of the claim is expounded upon by a few opportunists, and by the attention seeking mass media, seeking publicity for their miserable books, their "informational" programs, their documentaries, their tabloid stories.

3. The busybodies of society promulgate it further out of

a combination of pathological boredom and self righteous indignation.

  4. The fence sitters are silenced by the former group and remain so out of fear of being designated "witches."

  5. The panic eventually swells to such a size that it becomes unstable, and at least a few people in the first three groups die by their own sword, after which the panic is dismantled by its masters because it has become unprofitable.

  6. Some years or decades later the handful of people who bravely spoke out are recognized as sagelike despite merely recognizing obvious truth and being too stubborn or principled to ignore the situation.

  Thus we remember the rock stars of the 1980s as better than the tabloid spewers of the Satanic Panic, and the advocates of free thought as superior to Tipper Gore and the housewives of America who fought against metal, rap, and radio DJs. We remember the witchfinder as evil and the "witch" as good- and society will in due time remember the tiny minority of mavericks today as far better than the corporations, politicians, and "activists" seeking to destroy them. Fence seekers won't be remembered at all, because they are considered expendable dross by the witchfinder, and culpable idiots by the "witch." Todays witch is tomorrows reformist hero.

  Can you name a single neutral figure from the burning times, or a single tract that declared some permutation of "there are witches, but we should reconsider whether we're burning too many innocent people alive"? Or are they the ones the burning times truly burned to extinction, because they're so interchangeable, boring, uninspiring, and unlovable?

THE INVERSION OF FASCISM

The objections of certain "leftist" groups run the gamut but one of the most common claims I hear is that it's "okay" to persecute, deplatform, or even physically abuse the accused "witches" of the internet because they are "fascists" or because tolerating them will "lead to fascism."

I say first: Most people claiming this do not even know what fascism is.

Second: By adopting such an attitude, a person becomes no better than the Hollywood fascist they typically denote in their depictions.

Third: They are alluding to the tolerance paradox; the concept that a tolerant society is usurped by intolerance because of its lack of a defense mechanism. I counter that the real paradox is a *paradox of intolerance* because the only way these delusional authoritarians can think of to prevent intolerance is to adopt it and simply limit who it effects; but how is this different from the witchfinder and priest agreeing that *killing is wrong, unless it's a witch in league with Satan*?

The situations, the authoritarian claims, are apples to oranges; for intolerant extremists exist, and witches did not. They do? As I have said, I would personally vouch for some of your witches being uninvolved with modern day witchery. What say these societal dregs, incapable of doing anything for mankind except to destroy and suppress their intellectual superiors? Same as it ever was, most of the people they identify as extreme or hateful are anything but, and *even by their own self proclaimed standards* the accused are blameless. So why should we as a supposedly enlightened society tolerate *their* intolerance? For that is truly what it is; their resolution to see the world as ugly and bad, is making it ugly and bad, through their own malevolence or, in some cases, their own adopting of malevolent methods, even when they are themselves merely fooled and well meaning.

There are, of course, in the world, actual fascists- yes, they do exist. But much like "real" witches they are at odds most definitely with both the people accused and with the methods of accusation- the fascist of today is (when not being ironic and merely laughing at others' discomfort) a rare thing; more often, the term is bandied around like it is meaningless by the same people who claim it to be of great import. When someone states that another person is "like Hitler" or "a fascist" or "extreme" it is usually meaningless and sometimes an admission that the person is themselves "out there" socio-politically. These terms are most often used, it seems, by people who believe in some variant of hard line anarchism, communism, or who are merely generally violent and thuggish.

But because cognitive dissonance has kicked in, the average Antifa member is apparently acutely unawares that they are basically fighting on the behalf of billionaires and corporate politicians. The rudimentary fence sitter apparently never bothers to question this bizarre situation to any real degree either, and sees nothing strange in a self proclaimed anarchist (let alone a general leftist so-called) partnering with Silicon Valley billionaires and corporate news companies that get their marching orders from nations with severe human rights abuse problems. No, this is "perfectly rational" just like the notion of keeping society safe by imprisoning and tormenting old women because the cows in your village became ill and because she suffers from dementia.

Indeed, the real fascists- if we can use a mostly useless term- of the day, are arguably the corporate groups most responsible for these meaningless tidal waves of stupid propaganda. The corporate entities which encompass the legacy media, the tech giants, the "activistic" groups, and even some mainstream religions, are deeply authoritarian. Some of these same groups- political and otherwise- have promoted and promulgated literal warfare in which tens or hundreds of thousands of people have been killed. To see them claim, with a straight face, that some random person on the internet with a podcast is attempting to start a world war, is disgusting. To see the Catholic Pope, in his white robe, ramble about the need to snuff out intolerance, considering the past and present dictates of the Vatican, is hypocrisy manifest on a level not even his supposed adversary, Satan, could generate.

The amusing part is that the moralism spawned in these moral panics invariably benefits the persecutor. The witchfinder was free to sexually assault any female he wanted since he had to examine the "witch" completely naked, to "check her for the marks of the devil." This pernicious practice perhaps has a semi-modern form in our authoritarian red flag laws, which also have been fomented on a fake crime wave that doesn't even exist- after all we have to check up on those potential witches, make sure they're not causing any problems. Civil rights? Human rights? Who gives a damn? Not the politicians, not the "activists", and surely not the billionaires. They'll be rich and powerful no matter what happens; they don't care if the west adopts avowed communism so long as they're one of the party members that can import their alcohol and keep under-paying workers.

Indeed if fascism is said to exist today (or sociopolitical abuse, more generally) it exists in the form of the modern witchfinder- the politician, the priest, the "activist", the CEO. They're all potential witchfinders. Even then many merely sit on the fence, observing and doing nothing.

PURELY ANTI-AMERICAN AND UNPATRIOTIC

The burning times proper, predate the formation of the United States. This section perhaps therefore matters less, but it is of note in that most of the tech giants that exist today are in the United States; namely, In Silicon Valley.

The era of the Salem Witch Trials ended with the 17th century. None of those who founded the United States were alive back in that period, but they were the offspring of those who were. A cursory examination of some of the popular literature of the mid 1700s will show you an intrigue for the occult, an appreciation for the ideals of high antiquity, and a skepticism of then-mainstream religious forces that force me to believe that were Washington or Jefferson alive today, they'd be aghast at the kind of pseudoreligious attacks on their First Amendment being made today.

The first amendment was meant to limit the states ability to censor speech and written material; but we must go further, to the underlying *philosophical reason* why the amendment exists to understand its purpose. No reason for it can be established except by first understanding that it is the freedom itself which is notable. Were a man to attempt to silence another man, in those days, it could easily have ended in a duel to the death. Why then, if only state censorship mattered? The answer is very simple; any suppression of speech, thought, writing, was an abomination and would have been seen as disgusting and actively fought against. Indeed, such was the case early on, considering dissent against the alien and sedition act (and jailing of political dissidents resultant from it) was the underlying basis for Jefferson to be elected in the first place.

THE ILLUSION THAT IF YOU LICK THEIR BOOTS THEY WILL OVERLOOK YOU

Fence sitters were rudely awakened to reality, sometimes, during the persecutions of the witch trials. They figured that if they bought the witchfinder an ale and spoke well of him, that their wife wouldn't be sexually abused and pilloried and they wouldn't be hanged or drowned for their land holdings. Such was not the case; ignorance tends to be rather indiscriminate in its excesses and this is perhaps nowhere more evident than in a moral panic. Because polite society has been convinced that an existential threat to society exists, the most savage and abominable methods to disrupt the threat are employed to the great applause of the same people who may end up facing the same treatment if circumstances go awry.

I have seen this myself; in the last few years, more than a few commentators and media figures have had their careers ended or at least hazarded because they ran afoul of the same lynch mobs they helped to spawn. In Salem, it has been argued that the entirety of the trials which took place there were over property disputes. (I do not believe this, personally: I prefer the "moral panic based on exposure to ergotamine" theory myself.)

The governor of the state at the time stood by and did nothing as people were destroyed by persecution. That is, until his own wife was accused of witchcraft. The hysteria ended "fairly quickly." We may yet be at the end of our current witch hysteria (the one playing out largely on the internet- a scary, spooky place full of unknowns, if you're not part of the internet generation, at least!) as more and more perfectly mainstream political and corporate figures are hit by their own lynch mobs. This even extends to extremely "progressive" politicians. Bernie Sanders (A Senator from my own state, currently running to be the nominee for the Democrats in the 2020 presidential election) has been labeled a "sexist" by some fellow far leftists, even as he single mindedly fights against a wage gap that does not exist. He is a white male, and has thus also been ridiculed as the "old face" of politics by people who, they self-proclaim, are "anti-racist" (which is oddly often a code word for the actually racist.) This while he actually marched for Civil Rights, way back in the old days when the moral panic of the age involved communism and the USSR, instead of bloggers and people with video hosting websites.

No, the boot licking won't save you. Some people of course say "yes, I am out there maybe but I am not THAT edgy!" I counter with an obvious rational observation; if I take a blade and file the edge off, I don't remove the edge, I just make a new one which prior was not on the edge at all. This incremental erosion of what constitutes, "edgy" or "fringe" means that people who right now are not in the sights of the modern day witchfinder can easily find themselves there, along with those of us already persecuted merely for defending the same. Tragically, only a minority seems able to digest this oh-so-easy-to-grasp fact. I am not even entirely sure why, sometimes.

This erosion is equally in force simply because opportunists and fearmongers must of necessity always have a target to whine about. The former for profit, the latter because they are bored or merely fearful and looking for spooky things to be frightened of. When goblins and trolls went extinct they feared the criminally insane. When it was shown that criminal insanity was sparse, they feared wild animals. As wilderness was pushed back from society they began to fear exterior sociopolitical systems. As the cold war ended, everyone briefly worried about cults, until they were discredited entirely, and now they have decided that the witchcraft of today involves a webcam or a smartphone.

FIGHTING BACK

It is not enough to bemoan the authoritarians and the propaganda. It is necessary to say a few positive, encouraging words about what can be done to defend against tyranny and corporate abuse.

It may be difficult to convince the brainwashed that they have been lied to, but that is fundamentally the first step involved. We must seek the fence sitter and remind them that the authorities stand to gain materially from their lurid tales of armies of hate filled extremists, and that they even engineer such bigotry when able to fulfill the role. I have a real sneaking suspicion that corporate media firm staffers have occasionally designed their own stories by posting insane things anonymously on the internet- because where profit can be made and abuse commence, it usually does.

It is also good to defend one another. I note that many creators of internet content either never or only rarely defend others that have been abused. Sometimes, it is out of the same cowardice as those uninvolved centrists or "moderates" standing and gawking at the spectacle. For shame; don't they know they're also a "witch"? After all the others are pilloried, will anyone at all be left to defend them when their name is called to the gallows?

It is necessary to realize that truth is hidden by censorship. There is currently a push within the tech world to make everything cloud-and-app based, and therefore proprietary. Even archived material can be eliminated with the pressing of a button by some billion dollar corporation. It behooves people to store things locally that they do not wish to ever disappear, and to work on ways to promulgate material outside of the increasingly convoluted "internet of everything" which now encompasses what was once television and radio. The same internet that makes spreading and storing even the most obscure material (books come to mind!) is also a top-heavy centralized potential way for the same material to be Stalinized- that is, wiped out entirely forever. We must keep in mind that *even very popular materials can be forgotten eternally* if not protected. The world is down more than a few Homeric epics because people ignored this truth. The greatest song ever made might never be heard because the one bootleg recording made of it decades ago succumbed to an attic fire. Sad.

Finally we must remember that you get more flies with a spoonful of sugar than a gallon of vinegar. Most of the people participating in the persecution mean well but are fooled, or consider themselves "neutral" in order to absolve themselves of making any decisions at all. Remind the former that profit is made off suppression, and make them aware of the significant similarities between now and the burning times. Inform the latter that culpability for suppression extends to those who witness and comprehend it but do nothing. If anything, to comprehend it and do nothing is more evil than to participate if one judges their own motives to be righteous- the righteous one is more dangerous, but they at least do not intend evil.

THE TRUE EXTREMISM

In reality the true extremism and hate of our age is promulgated by these modern day witchfinders, the dregs, the intellectual light-weights and apologists of modern authoritarianism. Most of the time, these fools won't even debate the point because they are afraid to be exposed as the bought off, intellectually lazy parasites they are. When confronted, they scream endlessly about "attacks on the press" or how a person "is extreme" for not mollycoddling an establishment that is openly hostile towards them.

Yes, I am hostile in a way to the establishment; taken out of context (as statements normally are when reported on by the corporate gadfly media or its "activist" buddies) that could be taken as violent rhetoric- this pleases these corporate pests, even if such statements normally involve merely a pledge to fight against them on an intellectual, not physical, battlefield. When one does so, they are all that much more at risk, since the structure of the sociopolitical world was in part designed by these same ill-intended authoritarians.

The real extremism, as I see it, is the claim that everyone outside of what is deemed "normal" is therefore dangerous and that they should be unable to express themselves, defend themselves, conduct commerce or engage in banking, live a normal and dignified life, and expect the rudimentary chance to engage in that great capitalistic project that others get to engage in. It is extreme, that the people attempting to subvert this possibility are *themselves the ones most directly profiting materially from it*. And it is extreme when other supposedly intelligent people defend this abysmal abuse of the concept of authority. It is extreme to think that the communications infrastructure of the west is more endangered by some vloggers than by corporate oligarchs that control it and abuse it.

FALSE AUTHORITY IDENTICAL TO THE BURNING TIMES

The activistic groups of today are, as I stated prior, no different from those which existed many centuries ago, back when most people lived in single-room dirt floor dwellings poorly lit and heated by firewood, on rations of root crops and beer.

What is activism? The same subjectivists fond of saying "one mans terrorist is another mans freedom fighter" (thereby excusing literal violence in the name of some feigned benevolence, because they believe in the noble savage mythology of their forebears) never apply that logic to perfectly *non*violent "radicals" who merely wish to express themselves. In their haste to silence a supposed extremist they will simultaneously be fine silencing everyone associated with them. I will tell a little anecdote here that will interest some of you who are reading this manuscript:

Several years prior to me penning this little work, I was engaged in a debate which was streamed live on the internet; it was, mainly, billed as a debate between one Richard Spencer, and an internet persona called Sargon of Akkad, sometimes referred to by his given name Carl Benjamin. It felt slightly like I was tossed in as an afterthought, but an afterthought that attracted considerable fanfare; it seems the fact that I was willing to debate the subject (whether ethnonationalism was moral and/or feasible) without particular emotional attachment was deemed enjoyable and informative by many of the tens of thousands of people watching it.

Not long after. I was profiled by several far left groups as an "enabler of hate." This amused me since I was actually debating against what these groups initially deemed hateful. I was confused; but it was at that time that I began to realize the similarity between the witchfinders of the 17th century and the modern day moral crusades of the authoritarians; it *literally did not matter* that the claim was not just false but laughably false. It *did not matter* that anyone who watched the debate could tell I am not extreme in my views. It *did not matter* that I have never considered myself conservative, let alone "far right." All that mattered to the opportunists was money, and all that mattered to the busybodies is that reporting conformed to their predisposed reality; namely, that the internet was a place full of hate and extremism. The fact is that proper, fair reporting (something along the lines of "libertarian destroys debate opponent, undermines very central basis of claims of 'nonviolent' ethnonationalistic implementation") would not have generated as many views, not so much revenue, and would have been attacked by the moral crusaders, who would have called it "enabling hate" had this been the tagline.

It is through nonstop attack, extortion, and blackmail, that such groups operate. They defame with impunity and deplatform the figures which compete with their corporate backers with total immunity from the tech giants.

But remember, we few "witches" are the extreme ones. We're the problem of society. Just like Satanists, goths, wiccans, grunge rockers, metalheads, atheists, and heretics were before us.

I count myself lucky that I am on the right side of history, but I'll be damned if sometimes it isn't frustrating trying to get people to understand that not everyone called a witch practices witchery, and not every "extremist" has any extreme views. Sometimes they just pissed off a corporate billionaire who donated to the SPLC, or stood against a political platform embraced by the ADL. These "activists" operate on a principle directly opposite any reasoned definition of "academic rigor" too. Their "studies" are all obtuse legalese and are useless.

CONCLUSION: THERE AREN'T ANY BOGEYMEN

Here I conclude this little work. It is my hope that this has elucidated my thoughts on the topic of censorship to a degree impossible in a 15 or 20 minute video rant. It is my hope also that a century from now, some ivory tower academic will consult this work without giving me any credit; just as they will omit credit to many others who have made similar claims about our so-called "modern" time; for there are indeed others. Hindsight is 20-20. I require no magic wand to determine that a moral panic exists, and overlapping it with the burning times is no harder the comparing it with any other period of ignorance.

Believe it or not, there aren't any bogeymen. The specter of an army of hate filled, ugly, one-dimensional extremists is just that- a specter, a lonely, miserable ghost. When the light of truth is turned on, it is nothing more than your curtain blowing in a night breeze. You check your closet for goblins but there are only clothes. The wicked, twisted shadow on your wall moments before was nothing but the branches of a tree in front of the moonlight.

One dimensionality is always wrong. When you begin to see other people as beneath civic protection, as being undeserving of speaking their mind, when you have been led by others to submit that they should be silenced, beware! You have been fooled by propaganda; and in the 2010s, it is arguably as bad as it was in former times of sheer ignorance, the burning times being just one of a number. We must respect our fellow citizens at least to the extent that we allow them to speak out even if we deem them totally wrong. To not do so, is to risk disaster.

THE END

www.ingramcontent.com/pod-product-compliance
Lightning Source LLC
Chambersburg PA
CBHW050757250726

48662CB00005B/2277